THE COMPLETE

♥♥♥♥♥♥♥♥ ♥ ♥♥♥♥♥♥♥♥

Wedding Speech

Guide

THE COMPLETE

Wedding Speech

Guide

Andrew Byrne

NEW
HOLLAND

CONTENTS

Introduction

Common misconception: delivering a wedding speech, especially your first, is similar to leaping from an aeroplane with an umbrella for a parachute. The fact is, writing and giving a speech doesn't have to be like that at all.

There are two golden rules for delivering a well-received speech and actually enjoying the moment—preparation and practice. In clear, straightforward steps this book will guide you through planning, writing, and delivering your speech on 'the big day'. Whether you are the bride, groom, father of the bride, best man, friend, relative, the master of ceremonies or even a last-minute speaker, this guide is intended to help you deliver the speech you want to deliver.

Parts I and II will take you through the speech writing process: discovering what a person in your role normally says; deciding what you want to say; using a speech outline; practical writing tips; humor 'dos and don'ts' and writing and rehearsing the speech (using tested techniques).

Finally, in Part III all the secret ingredients for confidently and enjoyably delivering your speech on the day are revealed. Part III also takes you through warming-up, curing stage fright and projecting confidence in your voice.

Aided by techniques used in public speaking and by research and experience, this guide will help ensure that you and your speech are ready for the wedding day.

Your speech is an opportunity to tell loved ones how you feel about them on the most celebrated day in a couple's life. It's an honor and a privilege and should also be a pleasure. Allow yourself to enjoy that moment!

Part 1:

Speech Roles –
Contents and Advice

♥♥♥♥♥♥♥♥ ♥ ♥♥♥♥♥♥♥♥

'Ladies and gentlemen, I've been asked to say a few words …' And what will your words be? Well, your speech will be a balance of:

- what you want to say
- what your speech role may be expected to say.

A wedding has various speech roles. Some have traditional expectations (father of the bride, groom, best man). Others, being more recent additions, are far more flexible (bride, father of the groom, chief bridesmaid etc.). Furthermore, the style of your speech can be traditional or personalised, depending on your wishes and those of the bride and groom. Either way, understanding what someone in your role normally says will provide you with a head start before you even put pen to paper.

FINAL WORD ABOUT THE SPEECHES IN THIS PART

The speech roles and their contents listed here are a guide to what someone in that role would traditionally say. However, as weddings and their speeches are open to the wedding couple's personal touches and wishes, don't worry too much about stepping outside of tradition. The important thing is that you get out what you want to say and that the audience receives it as you intended.

Make sure you thank the right people and offer a toast and your best wishes to the married couple. Other than that, you have a free hand in making your speech what you want it to be—to say what you want to say.

CHAPTER I:

MC (Master of Ceremonies)

Most weddings have some form of MC (master of ceremonies) acting as circus ringmaster. The MC can either be a close friend or relative, the best man or even a professional MC. In some cases the married couple may even ask the father of the bride—it's their choice of course.

Besides their speaking role, the MC generally also ensures the reception location is ready before the guests arrive (more on this below). The MC acts as the reception's greeter and formally introduces the wedding party to the guests. When it is time for the speeches, the MC gets the attention of the guests by calling for silence. From then on, the MC's role is to introduce each speaker, as arranged.

WHO IS THE MC AT THE COMING WEDDING?
If the best man (or woman) is the MC

If the role of MC is being filled by the best man, he will be the first and last person to speak, with his best man speech coming at the very end. Other than that, he needs to follow the MC's tasks below.

If a professional MC is hired

Nowadays, you can hire a professional MC to organise and manage the speakers at your wedding, with the benefit that the MC is experienced—they know how to perk up the crowd and keep the speeches flowing, preventing any flat spots between speakers. However, some couples find the idea of using a stranger to speak at their wedding disconcerting or odd—it's all a matter of choice. If you decide to go for a professional MC, you should shop around and keep the following tips in mind:

- if possible, use an MC recommended by someone you trust

- interview the prospective MC and make sure you feel comfortable with them

- ask for references from previous clients.

A professional MC should be:

- confident, but not cocky

- able to listen to your requirements and not dictate them

- courteous and considerate.

PREPARATION

Unlike the other speakers, the MC's speech role is structured throughout the entire series of speeches. So, unless you're also delivering your own speech (such as the best man) you won't have to delve into stories about how the groom locked himself out of his car and then got arrested for trying to break into it. Of course, if such a story is a great link to introducing the next speaker (such as the police officer who arrested him) then go ahead and use it.

While you should stick to the speech writing rules in Part II, you have more of an opportunity to speak from the top of your head, as your main job is to introduce the next, and thank the previous, speaker.

MC'S ORGANISATIONAL TASKS

Although this is outside the area of speech writing, it is helpful to be aware of the other roles the MC traditionally performs. Depending on how the reception is organised by the wedding couple, the MC may also be called upon to ensure the reception location is ready for when the guests arrive. The MC's role may include:

- making sure the tables (including place names) are set as planned

- officially welcoming guests and formally introducing the wedding couple and party (upon arrival) to the guests

- ensuring the meal is punctual and drinks are flowing as per the wishes of the bride and groom

- managing the sequence of speeches (explained in detail below)

- organising the cutting of the wedding cake

- organising the bridal waltz (if required)

- gathering the guests for the throwing of the garter and the bride's bouquet

- organising the guests into a circle or bridal arch to farewell the bride and groom

- helping arrange the pack-up of items such as flowers and the wedding cake.

MC'S SPEECH TASKS

It's the MC's job to set a positive tone for the evening and the speeches to follow. As with speeches in general, if you are relaxed and enjoying yourself, the audience will pick up on this. That's half of your job done already.

Before the bridal party arrives

- Welcome the guests at the door and, once they are seated, introduce yourself and tell the guests that you will be their MC

- formally welcome the guests and thank them for coming

- if there are any additions to the reception (such as games) explain them now—keep the explanation clear and straightforward.

When the bridal party arrives

- Officially introduce the bridal party to the guests

- comment on the great day so far and make the guests feel involved by asking if they're having a good time remember that your job is to keep the joviality level up

- thank the bride and groom for asking you to be their MC.

After the meal is finished—the speeches

When the meal is finished, it's time for the MC to get the attention of the guests. Conversations around the tables will be in full swing by now. If the reception is large and noisy then bring your glass to the microphone. Tapping a glass for attention is not just tradition—it works. Once heads start to turn and voices lessen, it's time to speak. The nearest tables will settle down first and the rest should catch on.

The guests have eaten and should be feeling content and ready for the speeches. This is a crucial part in the speeches sequence. Like a warm-up act, you are setting the mood for the speakers to follow.

- Call for silence, for example, 'Ladies and gentlemen, if I could have your attention for a moment …'

- maybe offer that you hope they're well fed and happy

- once you have their attention you'll find there's still energy in the room from their conversations and you have about half a minute to make the most of that 'energy' after they fall quiet

- introduce the first speaker and when they've finished and have stepped down, you step up, thank that speaker and introduce the next person, and so forth

- if the wedding couple are happy for any emails or other messages (from people who couldn't attend) to be read out, you can do this after the main speakers are done—if you are also the best man, read them out before that speech

- again, if you are the MC and the best man, your speech should come at the very end (see Chapter 5 for the best man's speech role)

- if you are not giving a speech, end by thanking everyone once more and wishing them a wonderful night. If it's fine with the bride and groom, you could even end by proposing a final toast.

After the speeches

- With the speeches finished, announce the cutting of the cake (depending on the wedding couple's plans)

- traditionally, this is followed by announcing the bridal waltz—invite the newlyweds to take to the dance floor and follow up by inviting the rest of the wedding party to do the same

- after the wedding couple have had a chance to enjoy being alone on the dance floor (although some find it awkward, to be honest) invite the rest of the guests to hit the dance floor.

Time to go

- Arrange the single men for the throwing of the garter

- arrange the single women for the throwing of the bouquet

- when the bride and groom are ready to leave, get the attention of the guests and ask them to form a farewell circle or arch—this may take some organising and coercing (an electric cattle prod can be very useful!).

ADVICE

Pay attention to the mood of the guests. If you feel it may be slipping, try to pick up the pace and get them charged up again. One way of helping this (and increasing table activity) is to include some form of a game in the evening.

Pit each table against the rest. One idea is that they have to write the most amazing toast from the guests to the bride and groom. Getting each table to write a poem about the newlyweds is also a good technique. Even better is asking them to write it in the form of a limerick, which always results in hilarity. Seeing this in practice, I've noticed it adds a lot of energy to an evening. It encourages people to think up the nuttiest lines and breaks the ice for guests who don't know each other.

After the speeches, get each table to nominate a speaker who will step up and read their limerick to the guests. Be aware that there is always a risk of offending someone. If in doubt, do the rounds of the tables during the process and see how each table is going. Be delicate and diplomatic, but generally you'll find people are self-censoring.

For various reasons, reading out emails and other messages is not as popular these days. If a message is cordial yet unintentionally predictable, it may dull the energy of the guests. Discuss it with the wedding couple beforehand. If messages are being read out, make sure you limit them.

EXAMPLES

Although the MC has a great deal of freedom to ad lib, the following examples are designed to give you an idea of what is said. This will vary depending on the tone or formality of the wedding.

Before the bridal party arrives

Once the guests are seated. Ladies and gentlemen, it's with great delight that I welcome you here this evening to celebrate the wedding of [BRIDE] and [GROOM].

When the bridal party arrives

After asking the guests to be silent. Ladies and gentlemen! With your applause, please make very welcome the parents of the bride and the parents of the groom! [SAME FOLLOWS FOR THE REMAINDER OF THE WEDDING PARTY—BEST MAN, BRIDESMAIDS AND GROOMSMEN ETC.] Finally, please stand and welcome with your applause and cheers two very special, very happy, very newly married people—Mr and Mrs [SURNAME], the bride and groom!

After the meal is finished—the speeches

Tap a glass to get the guests' attention. Ladies and gentlemen, if I could have your attention for a moment … [WAIT FOR GENERAL SILENCE] thank you. I hope you enjoyed that fantastic meal and that all of you are content and full. I know I am—I've been trying to get out of my seat for ten minutes. [PAT YOUR STOMACH AND MAKE A FACE LIKE YOU'RE STUFFED. PAUSE FOR LAUGHTER]

If you have enjoyed the meal, then please join me in a round of applause for the staff here and in the kitchens. [PAUSE FOR APPLAUSE]

How are your hands? Warm? [PAUSE AND SMILE] Good—because I'm warming you up for the main part of this evening, the speeches! You may have spotted a few very nervous faces up here. [POINT TO MAIN TABLES] If you have, then at least you know who will be giving a speech.

If they think they're nervous, they should consider what it would have been like to be in [BRIDE]'s or [GROOM]'s shoes earlier today. Although I have to say I was really surprised to see how relaxed they were. I guess when you're in love and on cloud nine like they are today, what could possibly make you nervous? [PAUSE] Well, maybe an MC who rambles on and on … [PAUSE FOR LAUGHTER OR HECKLES] Actually, speaking of rambling, I'd like to introduce to you a man famous for his rambling mind, or is that raving mind? [PAUSE] Please put your hands together for the father of the bride! [SIMILAR STRUCTURE FOR THE REMAINING SPEAKERS]

After the speeches

Well I have to say those speeches made public speaking look easy. If any fool can do it, then the speakers tonight definitely proved it! [PAUSE]

Introduce the cake cutting as the bride and groom move across to the cake. Ladies and gentlemen, the wedding couple have a hankering for cake right now and I believe they brought their own along and are going to tuck into it right now. You're more than welcome to take as many photos of the cake with the newlyweds cutting into it, as you like!

Introduce the bridal waltz. I'd like to invite the wedding couple to take to the dance floor for the first dance of the evening, the bridal waltz. Please, give them your applause! [CONTINUE ON TO INVITE THE REST OF THE WEDDING PARTY AND, FINALLY, THE GUESTS TO DANCE]

Time to go

Ask the guests to come over for the throwing of the garter. If there are any single men in the room, please come forward. [BRIDE] is having a clothes sale but she's starting and ending the sale with a garter! Step right up and catch it if you can!

[SIMILAR AGAIN FOR THE THROWING OF THE BOUQUET]
Ask the guests to form a circle or arch to farewell the bride and groom. Thank you again for coming today and for your perseverance with me! I've never been heckled by such a polite crowd! But I want to thank you and hope that you've had a wonderful evening. [PAUSE]

Well, it's time to farewell Mr and Mrs [SURNAME] and wish them goodnight and good luck. If you could form a circle around the dance floor, the bride and groom will run around inside it so you can farewell them.

CHAPTER 2:

Father of the Bride

OVERVIEW

The first speech traditionally goes to the father of the bride. This stems from another old custom of the bride's parents paying for the wedding. Of course, today that's not always the case and the bride and groom often foot the bill (sometimes with parents also chipping in). But if you are the father of the bride and paying for the shindig, it's considered polite to let you speak first.

The father of the bride is asked to speak by the MC. You start your speech by thanking the guests for coming, and thanking those who have contributed to the wedding and those who have come a long distance to get there. Traditionally this is your opportunity to speak about your daughter and what she means to you—you're sharing how you feel handing her over to the care of her partner. At the same time, be aware that you should also be speaking on behalf of her mother (if she is not delivering a speech herself).

Be open and honest. This is a wonderful chance for you to tell your daughter, and all assembled, how you feel about her. Talk about her life—the ups and downs. The core element of your speech will be a particular story from her past. The anecdote is one that is special to you. It might encapsulate her entire character, reveal an aspect only a parent would remember with deep affection, or it might simply be a funny story—just make sure it doesn't require a lot of explaining.

If the anecdote is humorous, try to blend in some poignancy. Conversely, if your anecdote is emotionally stirring and beautiful, blend in some humor. Remember: the best speeches are a balance of both. Don't worry about coming across as 'all mushy'. This is a rare chance to be soppy and get away with it and not get gibed by your mates!

The other main purpose of your speech is to officially welcome your new son-in-law into your family. Maybe recall when you first met him or occasions you and he (and maybe his family) have shared together. Giving some marriage advice in a humorous way also goes down well (refer to the section in Part II on adding humor to your speech).

SPEECH CONTENTS

1   Thank the MC for his or her introduction If the MC is the best man, it's nice to thank him for the wonderful job he's done on the day.

2   Thank anyone who has contributed to the bill for the day.

3   The final thankyou is to the guests for coming and especially to those who have come a long distance.

4   Tell a story or anecdote from your daughter's life—it can either be one central one or a couple of shorter ones (work on blending them together).

5   Traditionally the father of the bride offers some words on love and marriage. Some people keep away from this—understandably they don't want to appear to be teaching the groom to suck eggs. However, there's nothing wrong with offering some warm words about marriage.

6   Say some words about the groom. What do you think of him and his family (especially his parents)? Is there something about him that has struck a chord with you? Tell him.

7   Don't forget to include your partner, especially when wishing the new bride and groom a happy future together and then thanking people.

8   Finally, end your speech with a proposal of a toast to the bride and groom.

ADVICE

If there is no MC and some guests may not know you, you should introduce yourself.

If there is anyone who could not make it to the wedding (such as for serious health reasons) and they are close to the bride or groom, it's a polite touch to mention their absence and wish them well.

If there has been a recent death in the family, it's also considered fitting to remember them on this day (especially if they were close to your daughter). Although for some it can be an emotionally difficult or sensitive issue to broach, it can also be touching. (More advice on this in Part II.)

EXAMPLE

[TURN TO MC] Thank you [MC] for that flattering introduction and for the wonderful job you've done so far.

[TURN TO GUESTS] Ladies and gentlemen, the fabulous memory of today will remain with both myself [TURN TO WIFE] and [WIFE'S NAME] for the rest of our lives. It was simply a perfect and beautiful day. Knowing [BRIDE] and [GROOM] as I do, it's not surprising it turned out as well as it did. They put a great deal of preparation into it. I'd also like to take this opportunity to thank [NAMES OF THOSE WHO HELPED PLAN OR FUND THE WEDDING] for their deeply appreciated contribution to making this day what it was—and still is.

[TURN TO BRIDE] [BRIDE], you look absolutely stunning today, darling. Your mother and I are incredibly proud of you.

[TURN TO GROOM] [GROOM], you're a wonderful person and we're very honored to welcome you into our family. [BRIDE] thinks the world of you and I understand why. Seeing you both today, just … well, it just seems completely right.

[TURN TO GUESTS] Forgive this 'old' man if you can, but it feels like not so long ago that [BRIDE]'s loud music was thumping through the house. It used to drive me mad, that racket. Of course, being a teenager at the time she knew this and as a result turned the volume up even higher. Little did I realise back then that it would be because of her love for that same God-awful racket that she would meet [GROOM]. Maybe that music isn't so bad after all [PAUSE]. Actually, no—it is bad. However, I'll give it one good point—it was the first thing you both found in common.

Yesterday, the list of items [BRIDE] and [GROOM] have in common was much greater and much deeper than when they first met. As of today, they have one more thing in common—they're married to each other.

Of course, the things we have in common are great, but a man and a woman can also have their differences. And when it comes to marriage, I think these differences too often get a bad name. Now this is where I give some marital advice—I should know what I'm talking about, because [WIFE'S NAME] has been giving me marital advice since before we married! [PAUSE FOR LAUGHTER].

As I was saying—I think we often give a bad name to these differences between a man and a woman or between any two people. Living happily with our commonalities is easy; living happily with our differences may seem difficult, but it can be wonderful in its own way.

[TURN TO BRIDE AND GROOM] I think one of the many keys to a happy marriage is to cherish those differences, because they're just as much a part of the person you are in love with as those things you have in common. [PAUSE] This evening I see two extraordinary people who are already on that road; they already have a wonderful respect for each other's differences. Why? [PAUSE] Because they're two people who have a great ability to let their hearts shine honestly.

So, even though I don't think the wedded couple need me to wish them happiness for their future—I can see it there in them already—on behalf of [WIFE'S NAME] and myself, we both wish you a very long, healthy and incredibly happy future together.

[TURN TO GUESTS] And never the one to pass up a toast, and no toast is more worthwhile than this, please be upstanding and join me [RAISE YOUR GLASS] in a toast [TURN TO BRIDE AND GROOM AND RAISE GLASS] to the bride and groom!

CHAPTER 3:

Groom

OVERVIEW

The groom's speech traditionally comes after the father of the bride's. If the bride is not going to be giving her own speech, remember that your speech is given on her behalf as well. The groom's speech is also used to thank those who have contributed to the wedding either financially (such as parents, if the father of the bride hasn't already thanked them) or through their assistance (the best man, groomsmen, bridesmaids, usher, flower girls and pageboys etc.).

Your speech is an opportunity to reflect on the event that has brought the guests together on the day. (Well, they've turned up, so the least you could do is tell them why they're there!) You can do this by relating how you and your wife first met. What went through your mind? What about the early days? First meal together? The day you (or she!) popped the question?

SPEECH CONTENTS

1   If your wife is not going to be delivering her own speech, then it's a good idea to start your speech with, 'My wife and I ...' This is a nice technique for drawing the guests in. After all, this is the very first opportunity amongst family and friends to use this phrase—a fitting place if ever there was one.

2   If you have been introduced to the guests by the MC, thank the MC for the introduction and for doing a great job.

3   Thank the father of the bride for his kind words and respond in kind to any compliments he has given you in his speech. (See the 'Advice' section below for more on this.)

4   Thank the guests for coming—if the father of the bride hasn't already thanked those who came from a distance to get to the wedding, then you should.

5   Thank everyone for their generous wedding gifts.

6   It's always warm and polite to sincerely congratulate the bride's parents on doing a wonderful job of bringing her up.

7   Comment on how the day has gone so far (maybe use it as a link to the story of how you and your new wife first met).

8   Explain how you and your wife met. Who made the first move? Who proposed to whom?

9 Add in any humorous stories about your life together so far. If your new wife is not going to deliver a speech, make sure you devote a large part of your speech to her—tell her how you feel about her and what she means to you.

10 For a flow effect, turn your speech's direction towards the best man (especially if his speech is directly after yours). Thank him for accepting the role (and also if he is the MC) and maybe tell the guests you're dreading what he's going to say (which you probably will be).

11 Thank the bridesmaids (and groomsmen) on behalf of yourself and your new wife. Offer them a toast from both of you.

12 And finally, offer a toast to your beautiful wife—although this isn't traditional, it gives the groom a very precious moment to step back with all those assembled and honor his new bride. On the occasions I have seen a toast from the groom to his bride, the response has been touching.

ADVICE

If you have been introduced by the MC, listen out for any dig or joke he has flung at you in his introduction. Before you step up to speak, try to think of a nice comeback to get him with. Character assassination of the groom is traditional at most weddings, so be prepared to give some back! Defend yourself, man!

If the father of the bride said that he had great faith in you or that he and his wife are proud to have you as a son-in-law then reply in kind. For example, 'Thank you for your kind words [FATHER-

IN-LAW]. I'm proud to be your son-in-law and I won't let you or [MOTHER-IN-LAW] down …'

When you are congratulating the bride's parents on how well they've brought up their daughter, your wife, see it from their point of view. They've loved her, worked hard for her, fed her, put her through school and supported her. Every parent wants to know if they've done the best they could. Hearing this from the groom (their new son-in-law) means a great deal to them, so, let them know.

If the best man is not yet married, remind him that whatever he says about you tonight, you too have a long and vengeful memory! It's a case of 'he who laughs last' and all that … I've witnessed this kind of humorous sparring and it has added a real laugh to the speeches. One of them almost became a comedy show, which also serves as a warning not to let things get too carried away.

If someone couldn't attend the wedding because of illness, mention them and wish them a speedy recovery. Depending on the circumstances (and the audience) maybe crack a joke about where they 'really' might be.

If either of your, or the bride's, parents have passed away, consider mentioning them in the speech. (For advice on this subject, refer to the section in Chapter 11 called 'Discussing family or friends who have passed away'.)

Some grooms' speeches also include a thank you to his own parents and/or any extra close family or friends who've helped him in life.

Another idea that is sometimes used is for the groom and the bride to make a speech together. Of course, this involves a lot of cooperation (what an opportunity to test your marital skills!). A joint speech would involve all the elements of the groom's speech contents (above) and a choice from the bride's speech contents. It can add a special touch to the speeches and give extra meaning to 'speaking for the both of you'. The amount of preparation and cooperation involved in a joint speech is probably why this technique is rarely used (you'll probably be busy enough just arranging the day itself). However, if you and your bride-to-be find the idea appealing, give it a go.

EXAMPLE

[TURN TO FATHER OF THE BRIDE] Thank you [FATHER OF THE BRIDE] for your kind words and for having me in your family—it's an honor for me as well. [PAUSE] I'd also like to thank you and congratulate you and [MOTHER OF THE BRIDE] on bringing up such a loving, caring, intelligent and beautiful daughter as [BRIDE]. I promise to deserve the kind things you just said about me.

[TURN TO GUESTS] Ladies and gentlemen, my wife and I [PAUSE] would like to sincerely thank you all for sharing this day with us and for your generous gifts. I also want to thank [MC] for his [OR HER] work and entertainment. [PAUSE] I'd also like to thank [BEST MAN] for keeping me calm and focused today, unlike the bucks' night when he kept me legless and blurry-eyed. [PAUSE FOR LAUGHTER] Really though—you've been great. I say these nice things to you now because I know your speech will be full of nice things about me later! Won't it? [PAUSE FOR LAUGHTER]

[TURN TO BRIDESMAIDS AND GROOMSMEN] I'd also like to thank the groomsmen and, of course, the stunning bridesmaids. Their help has made a real difference to our preparations.

[TURN TO YOUR PARENTS] Thank you too to my parents for all you've done for me. [PAUSE] It's terrible in a way, now I'm married

I can't bring my washing home for mum to do, and because I believe in equality, I can't leave it for [BRIDE] to do.

I have to learn how to do it. [FAKE SOB] Oh, I might seem happy on the outside but inside I'm crying fabric softener tears! [PAUSE FOR LAUGHTER]

But it's worth it and I've left my very best thankyou to last. My thankyou is to that beautiful woman you may have seen standing next to me today who looks so absolutely stunning. [TURN TO BRIDE] Thank you [BRIDE] for having me as your husband; for filling me with sunlight. Thank you for being the wonderfully, funny, caring, enchanting and gorgeous woman that you are. [PAUSE] I love you.

[TURN TO GUESTS] The fact is I loved her from the start. But, being younger then, I was too dumb to notice for about a week. I must have made a great impression on her because after we met, [BRIDE] went away for a week's holiday with her sister! [PAUSE] During that short span, I didn't realise what was wrong with me until [BEST MAN] began reminding me to eat and to stop staring at the clouds like a happily medicated patient.

Maybe love is a healthy sickness wrapped up with its own cure. [PAUSE] That bizarre ailment called love—it would make you do anything for her. It makes her happiness crucial to yours. Maybe that's what they mean about two becoming one. [PAUSE] That's why I look forward to our life together so much. [PAUSE]

Well, before I slip into that lovesick stupor let me once again thank all of our wonderful wedding party. Please, join with us in a traditional and well-deserved toast to the groomsmen and the bridesmaids.

CHAPTER 4:

Bride

OVERVIEW

Today, it's not uncommon for a bride to step up and give a speech. Unlike the traditional speakers (father of the bride, groom and best man) the bride's speech has no huge expectation attached to it. As a result, the contents of your speech are completely what you want them to be.

So, if it's not traditional for you to give a speech, why would you? Well, it is also your special day so why not? It's an opportunity to respond to your husband's speech, to speak about what your husband means to you and to personally and publicly thank those who've made the day possible. The speech contents below are intended to give you a better idea of what you might say. Again, add or subtract from it to suit you.

SPEECH CONTENTS

1   Thank those who've helped you prepare for the day—the groom should have already thanked the wedding assistants in his speech, but there's nothing wrong with you also thanking them if you wish.

2   If your father has given the father-of-the-bride speech, then here's a nice opportunity for you to express to both him and your mother how you feel about them. Thank them for their support and for all they've done for you.

3   Describe your relationship with your parents and with any brothers or sisters you may have—humorous family stories always go down well.

4   Talk about the groom's parents—in traditional speeches, the groom's parents don't get a huge mention (except for in the father of the bride's speech) so why not thank them for bringing up their son so well and for welcoming you into their family?

5   You may have a funny anecdote about your husband, which provides some more room for humor. It could be from when you first met or early dates or even something that occurred during the wedding preparations. He may have already covered these areas in his speech, but not this particular story.

6   Jokes aside, this is also a chance for you to tell your husband what he means to you in front of a room full of people who also mean a lot to you.

7   To finish up, you could use a very recent addition to wedding toasts—thanking the guests by toasting them on behalf of the wedding group.

ADVICE

If there is anybody special, such as a close friend, who has helped you during your life up to this point (for example during tough times) then this is a good opportunity to thank them.

Sometimes, the bride may wish to deliver a speech if her father is not present. This essentially means she's filling in the father of the bride's speech role. If this is the case, also refer to the father of the bride chapter (Chapter 2).

EXAMPLE

I'd like to thank my parents for all they've done for me and to thank [GROOM]'s family for welcoming me so warmly. I also want to thank the wedding party for making all the hard work seem so much easier.

[TO GUESTS] As you know, it's not traditional for the bride to make a speech. But I grew up with four older sisters, and as [GROOM] knows, I'm never shy about getting my word in!

[PAUSE FOR LAUGHTER] That's probably why I was stunned when [GROOM] proposed. There we were, sitting back on a quiet secluded beach watching the waves roll in—just happy.

Then [GROOM] gets up, but he doesn't, he just rests on one knee, that 'bended knee' pose. Before I could push him into the sand—which I would have done normally—he holds out a ring and asks, 'Why don't we go and get married?' [PAUSE]

I think the sun set before I finally answered him. [PAUSE] Not because I wasn't sure what to say and not because my mind was spinning. [PAUSE] I took my time because I wanted to enjoy that moment—to savour what it meant.

When I finally did answer, the sun was just a lip on the edge of the world. And how did I answer him? There, in that remote and beautiful place? There, with poor [GROOM] still on his bended knee starting to lose his circulation? [PAUSE] My 'yes' came out in a flood of tears and I was a total mess … I was a mess and I was happy. But I'm glad I hung onto that special moment in our life—I wanted it to last. I wasn't being cruel, I was recording and relishing it all.

And it was worth it. [GROOM] is more than worth it. When I say that I'll love him my whole life it's not because it's easy to say such a thing—I say it because I know it's true. [PAUSE] That's what brought us here today [TURN TO GUESTS] and what brought you here too. So let me thank you all for coming and making our day extra special.

CHAPTER 5:

Best Man

OVERVIEW

For humor, the best man's speech is the most anticipated (sorry to scare you). If you're a natural showman, you'll probably lap this role up. If not, you'll still enjoy yourself more than your current nerves and apprehension are allowing you to believe is possible. Fear not—although the best man's speech is usually expected to get a laugh from the guests, people aren't going to expect the delivery and material of a stand-up comedian.

If you're also acting as the MC, you'll already have warmed up a little, so remain relaxed and enjoy yourself. Remember, as best man, you are also speaking on behalf of the rest of the wedding assistants (the groomsmen, bridesmaids, ushers, etc.).

The role of best man today is sometimes (although not commonly) carried out by a best woman. If this is the case, follow the same contents, where relevant.

SPEECH CONTENTS

1   If you are not also doubling up as the MC, thank the MC for their introduction.

2   Thank the groom (and bride if she has also spoken before the best man) for their kind words about the wedding assistants. Also thank them for the honor of being best man.

3   Traditionally the wedding couple give gifts to the wedding party. On behalf of them and yourself, thank the wedding couple for these gifts. Maybe joke that the gifts will not act as a bribe and stop you from making fun of the groom.

4   Tell a couple of funny stories and anecdotes about the groom. If you and the groom grew up together, touch on} that—you could even run your stories as if you were recapping his life. Sometimes funny things happen during the wedding preparations and of course the bucks' night tends to have plenty of fuel in it too.

5   If you have any humorous anecdotes about the bride, include them too (unless a bridesmaid is going to be making a speech covering the bride's past).

6   If you have some funny stories, balance them with something poignant and touching. Don't be afraid to express your friendship.

7   On behalf of yourself and the wedding party, give the bride and groom your best wishes for their future together.

8   Conclude your speech by asking the guests to raise their glasses in a toast to the bride and groom.

ADVICE

During your speech, make a point of addressing the wedding couple directly. Do the right thing by the bride and steer clear of the groom's previous relationships unless you're absolutely certain it will be received well. In any of your funny anecdotes about the groom, if there is a prop you can use, use it. Props enhance the hilarity of jokes or funny stories, especially those with a history such as props from childhood (a toy car, school bag or a letter they wrote as a child). (Refer to the 'Using humor' section in Part II for more information.)

If you are already married and your best man was the current groom, use this as an opportunity for revenge if he really dug into you at your wedding. Revenge, as they say, is a dish best served cold (followed by a very sinister laugh!).

EXAMPLE

Ladies and gentlemen, before I start, I'd like to take this opportunity on behalf of my fellow partners in wedding assistance crime, the bridesmaids and groomsmen, to thank [BRIDE] and [GROOM] for their kind words and their considerate gifts. Although the book you gave me looks exactly like the one I loaned [GROOM] back in 2012. [PAUSE FOR LAUGHTER]

[TURN TO BRIDE AND GROOM] Personally though, I want to thank you both for asking me to be your best man. I think you're insane, but thank you—it's a real honor.

[TURN TO GUESTS] I'm sure you've all been waiting for my speech because as you know, the best man has a great job. I get to make [GROOM] squirm for a few minutes. Now, if he starts squirming, don't feel sorry for him—he squirms like that a lot. It's a physical defect, but [BRIDE] tells me it doesn't bother her at all for some reason! [PAUSE FOR LAUGHTER]

To be honest, despite what you might be expecting, I won't be telling you about the time [GROOM] walked around for a whole day at school with his fly open. No big deal you may think— not if you're wearing undies, which he wasn't. [PAUSE FOR LAUGHTER] That means I won't tell how the whole school knew about it by the end of the day. And if I don't tell you that, then I won't tell you that's how he got stuck with the nickname of 'Draughty' for years. [PAUSE]

So I won't be telling tales like that. Instead I'll explain the kind of guy [GROOM] is by way of demonstration. [PAUSE] [GROOM] is sensitive, caring and nurturing. [PRODUCE OLD TEDDY BEAR FROM UNDER LECTERN] See? Look at the good condition this teddy is in. Scary, isn't it? And do you know where I found this? In his bedroom! [PAUSE FOR LAUGHTER]

So it's not surprising he found a match in [BRIDE]. She is just as caring and nurturing as he is. Worse still, she's even more of a lunatic than he is. [PAUSE] Straitjacket or not, I think they both look fantastic today. In fact I think they will look fantastic even when they're old and wrinkly. They'll look fantastic because they'll still be in love. [PAUSE]

With that said, on behalf of the bridesmaids, groomsmen and myself, I'd like to wish [BRIDE] and [GROOM] a life together even better than [GROOM]'s teddy's, a life that is long, filled with laughter, good health and fortune.

Again, on behalf of the bridesmaids, groomsmen and myself please join us in proposing a toast to the bride and groom!

CHAPTER 6:

Mother of the Bride

OVERVIEW

Similar to the bride, although it's not traditional for the mother of the bride to deliver a speech, there is nothing wrong with her doing so. Your speech is very flexible, so if there's something special you want to say about your daughter and the man she has just married, this is a perfect opportunity to do so.

SPEECH CONTENTS

1   Thank the MC for the introduction.

2   Talk about your daughter and the relationship you have with her.

3   Relate any significant or humorous memories of her as a child.

4   Talk about the groom and what you think of him and his family.

5   Maybe provide some motherly advice with a balance of sincerity and humor. It should come across as loving advice and your wishes for their future together.

6   As the groom's new mother-in-law, why not use that
      unfairly infamous title to crack a joke? Threaten him (not
      seriously, obviously!). You could even scare the lad by
      promising to visit every second day, then tell him that his
      mother will be visiting every other day. This 'motherly
      conspiracy' can be a very funny addition to the speeches.
      If the mother of the groom is also giving a speech then
      work such a trick out with her beforehand when you're
      both writing your speeches.

7   Whatever you frighten him with, end it on a sincere and
      friendly note, welcoming him into your family.

8   Finish up by wishing both of them a happy and healthy
      future together.

ADVICE

If for any reason you are filling the father of the bride's speech role, you
should use that role's speech contents (refer to the relevant chapter).

If there is no MC and some guests may not know you, then
introduce yourself. You could do this casually by saying something
such as, 'As [BRIDE]'s mother …' To add some humor, maybe even
say, 'As [BRIDE]'s long-suffering mother …'

EXAMPLE

It's not often a mother gets the undivided attention of her
children without having to threaten to send them to their room.
Of course, it's been a very long time since I've had to use that
phrase on [BRIDE]. Just like it's been a long time since I read her

fairytales at bedtime but it feels like yesterday—in fact, I think it was yesterday! [PAUSE FOR LAUGHTER]

I have to say, [BRIDE] was generally a well-behaved child. I say 'generally' because when she did get out of hand, oh boy, did she put up a fight! From the start [BRIDE] was the kind of person who stood her ground.

I remember a few staring matches we had, especially over Brussels sprouts—she absolutely hated them! On one occasion I told her she couldn't leave the table until she had eaten them. She refused and cheekily told me she'd stay until … [TURN TO BRIDE] what were the words, dear? [PAUSE] Until they 'rotted on the plate'. [PAUSE FOR LAUGHTER] [TURN TO GUESTS] She went on to describe what they would look like and smell like when they finally rotted. It was a disgusting picture! [PAUSE] When she finished her description we just sat there staring each other down … for nearly half an hour. [PAUSE] So who won? Hard to say, really. In the end she ate one of the two sprouts while putting on a face as if she were eating worms. It was threat, then negotiation and a diplomatic solution. [PAUSE]

When I think back on that now, I look upon her with pride. I knew then and there that [BRIDE] was never going to be someone to boss around. At the same time she had a deeply caring heart, especially for people feeling down, so it's no surprise she ended up being a physical therapist.

[TURN TO GUESTS] Ah, children. Predictable and unpredictable. They can drive you up the wall but they can make you teary when you think of how much they mean to you. Then suddenly, they find a certain someone to love and who loves them, in this case, [GROOM].

When [PARTNER] and I first met [GROOM], you could see they had each other figured out already. They looked like they'd been together for decades. [GROOM] is a kind, warm and considerate man. It's not surprising really, especially since we've gotten to know his parents, [MOTHER AND FATHER OF THE GROOM]. [PAUSE]

As I said, your daughter finds someone to love and who loves her in return and, before you know it, they're making their own home. It doesn't make me sad, though. [BRIDE] has grown into a woman who I'm incredibly proud to know.

[TURN TO BRIDE] And if I don't get to tell her to go to her room or read her fairytales these days, maybe I can at least say this: [BRIDE], go be with your groom and live happily ever after.

CHAPTER 7:

The Chief Bridesmaid

OVERVIEW

The chief bridesmaid is lucky with her speech. Unlike the best man's speech, yours is not constrained by traditional contents such as thanking everybody including the cashier at the garage pay booth. Instead, while the best man gets to have a bit of fun at the groom's expense, you get to have fun at the bride's. Depending on how long you've known her, you probably have some great stories and there's also nothing wrong with offering a little helpful 'marital advice'.

SPEECH CONTENTS

1   Thank the MC for the introduction.

2   Thank the bride and groom for inviting you to speak.

3   Give a humorous description of your relationship with the bride.

4   Describe her as a person (balance it with humor and sincerity).

5   If you have any funny stories about the bride or about the bride and groom together, dish it out.

6   Offer the bride some advice on marriage—again this can be humorous.

7   Finish up by telling her what she means to you and wish them both a happy future together.

ADVICE

Blend the contents into each other. For example, your description of the bride as a person could lead into a funny story you have about her past. Although the golden rule concerning jokes about the bride is that they should be made with extreme caution, you have the added advantage of a special relationship with her, so you can get away with a bit more.

EXAMPLE

I'd like to thank [BRIDE] and [GROOM] for asking me to be the chief bridesmaid and actually inviting me to speak. I've known [BRIDE] since we first started school. It was a friendship set to last from that first day.

As you know, the first day of school affects people in different ways. Some are silent with shock. Some are too busy picking their noses and gazing around to realise what they've just been thrown into. Others find it all too much and sit there balling their eyes out calling for their mummies.

[BRIDE] and I were part of that last group. Our mothers had probably explained what this 'school' place was but, you know, they might as well have been telling us we were going to Mars— well it certainly felt like that to us. There we were, two little strangers sitting next to each other, crying our heads off in a new and scary world. [PAUSE] Then [BRIDE] looked at me and I looked at her. She stopped crying, put her hand on my shoulder and said, 'It's okay. We're in school.' [PAUSE]

That says an awful lot about [BRIDE]. You could be lost at night in a beaten up old hire car in the mountains of Laos and she'd smile reassuringly and say, 'It's okay. We're in Laos.' Which really happened when we went backpacking around South-East Asia six years ago! [PAUSE FOR LAUGHTER] Sure, the actual advice of where we were didn't really help, but hearing her say it as if this was all perfectly normal did. She's one in a million. [PAUSE]

That's why when [BRIDE] told me she and [GROOM] were going to get married I thought, 'That figures!' [GROOM] is also one in a million. Now they're two in a million and I'm honored to count them as friends.

[TURN TO GROOM] [GROOM], I'm sure you'll look after my [BRIDE] and I know she'll look after you. I hope you'll have a wonderful life together, and if the road gets difficult or bumpy along the way, as marriages can, just say to each other, 'It's okay. We're married!'

CHAPTER 8:

Mother of the Groom/ Father of the Groom

OVERVIEW

When there is an opportunity for either the mother or father of the groom to say a few words, it provides a nice opening to not only express what the wedding means to them but to welcome the bride into their family. The speech is basically the same whether the mother or father is delivering it.

You could rely on aspects of your role as mother or father to flavor your speech, as each of you has your own gender's take on life, marriage and the proper position of the toilet seat after use!

SPEECH CONTENTS

1 Thank the MC for the introduction.

2 If the father of the bride has already thanked those who contributed to the cost or organisation of the wedding, there is really no need to thank them again—instead offer some warm words to the father and mother of the bride.

3   Talk about your son—tell the guests any memorable stories that define his character (they could be humorous or poignant). Most of all tell your son how you feel about him.

4   Sincerely welcome the bride into the family.

5   Talk about your new daughter-in-law. What impression has she made on you? What effect has she had on your son?

6   Finish up by wishing the happy couple a wonderful life together.

ADVICE

If there is no MC and some guests may not know you, introduce yourself.

A humorous technique called the 'motherly conspiracy' was mentioned in the mother of the bride speech (see Chapter 6 for more details). This conspiracy is a way of linking a joke between both mothers but it could also be arranged to fit any jokes the fathers come up with.

EXAMPLE

Ladies and gentlemen, for those of you who don't know me, I'm [GROOM]'s dad. You may have recognised me by the bags under my eyes. [PAUSE] Some people don't like having wrinkles, but I don't mind them. In fact I'm proud of these bags under my eyes. I like to think of them as medals earned in the line of duty. [PAUSE]

That duty started on [DATE OF GROOM'S BIRTH]—the day [GROOM] was born. My comrade-in-arms was my wife [WIFE'S

NAME] who eventually became general! [TURN TO WIFE] Well, my love, you deserved it, after all you carried him and went through the labour, something I certainly couldn't have done!

[TURN TO GUESTS] When [GROOM] was born, I had no real idea how long my parenting tour of duty would last. But after six months of changing a baby and endless laundry I knew the campaign would go on for a long, long time. As [GROOM] grew older, the whole idea of an end to this tour seemed to vanish and eventually, I got to the stage where I never wanted it to end. [PAUSE]

I got to see our son grow from a kindergarten terror who looked up women's dresses to a young child who seemed completely fascinated by the world around him. Of course my admiration had its limits, especially when he tried making his own rocket fuel when he was eight. [PAUSE FOR LAUGHTER AND TURN TO GROOM] Oh, you remember, do you? Good!

[TURN TO GUESTS] You see, we used to have this old barbecue and [GROOM] thought it would make the perfect launching pad for his rocket with his new 'rocket fuel'.

While [WIFE'S NAME] and I were gardening out the front of the house, [GROOM] had fueled and primed his rocket on his barbecue launching pad ... right next to the back window of the house. [PAUSE] We didn't know that his experimental fuel was made out of everything with a 'highly-flammable' label on the side. [PAUSE]

The first thing we heard was the biggest bloody bang you've ever heard in your life, followed by glass breaking and the sound of the barbecue going through the back door! [PAUSE FOR LAUGHTER] Well, as you can see, he lived, although we could have strangled him. Still, even then I didn't want this tour of duty that is parenting to end. [PAUSE]

[TURN TO BRIDE] Then one day years later [GROOM] comes home with this brilliant girl. Since then we've gotten to know [BRIDE] and I don't think [WIFE'S NAME] or I could say enough good things about her. We couldn't ask for a more honest and charming daughter-in-law.

[TURN TO FATHER AND MOTHER OF THE BRIDE] The same can be said for her wonderful parents whom, it's a pleasure to say, we have become great friends with.

[TURN TO GROOM] Son, you've found yourself a terrific wife, friend and partner in life and your mum and I are incredibly happy for you both. We wish both of you the very, very best for your future. [PAUSE]

[TURN TO GUESTS] As for my tour of duty ... well, no parent ever stops being a parent, do they? Not really. [PAUSE] So when I look in the mirror in the morning, at these medals, [POINT TO BAGS UNDER EYES] I just think about [GROOM]. I think about all the years we've spent together. I think of the man he's become, whom I admire so much [PAUSE] and I also think about that bloody rocket fuel sometimes too! [PAUSE FOR LAUGHTER]

No matter what, he still makes me smile. So, on behalf of [WIFE] and I, good luck to you both for your new life together.

CHAPTER 9:

Close Friend or Relative

OVERVIEW

Sometimes a close friend or relative of either the bride or groom is invited to make a speech. This may be because they have a particularly rich relationship with that person. (Note: if you are filling in for the father of the bride, base your speech on that role instead of this one.)

As a person dear to one (or both) of the wedding couple, you are essentially free to say what you feel about them, who they are and what this day means to you as a result. So, you can put your heart on your sleeve.

SPEECH CONTENTS

1   Thank the MC for introducing you.

2   Briefly explain who you are and your relationship with the wedding couple.

3   Thank the bride and groom for inviting you to speak.

4   Discuss what the bride or groom and, as a result, what the day means to you.

5   If you have any particularly strong memories of the bride or groom, or funny anecdotes, tell them. You could use such a story as a humorous warning to their new spouse.

6   Talk about their new spouse and how they seem together.

7   Maybe give them some light-hearted marital advice.

8   Finally, give them your best wishes for their future together.

ADVICE

Whatever you choose to say, remember that your words are intended to provide another view of the person you're speaking of.

EXAMPLE

Thank you [BRIDE] and [GROOM] for asking me to speak tonight, your wedding night.

[TURN TO GUESTS] As [BRIDE]'s aunt, seeing her with [GROOM] today was one of the loveliest sights of my entire life. I really mean it. [PAUSE] I've known [BRIDE] since she was born and the partner she has found in [GROOM] makes absolute sense.

[BRIDE] loves messiness. [GROOM] likes things to be orderly. [BRIDE] hates cooking but cooks like a chef. [GROOM] loves cooking but, as he once told me, he cooks like a mechanic. So, what is it that brings these opposites together? Is love that strong? [TURN TO BRIDE AND GROOM] It obviously is. [PAUSE]

[TURN TO GUESTS] But I also think every marriage has a certain thing that makes two particular people click. In the case of [BRIDE] and [GROOM], they aren't only husband and wife or lovers or partners—they're also best friends. [PAUSE]

They are two people who might disagree on this or that, but never let anything get between the bond they've created. [PAUSE] That's why today was one of the loveliest sights of my life—I saw harmony. And if [BRIDE] and [GROOM] can walk through life and marriage with that harmony, then, as I think you can already see, they are set for a beautiful life together. [TURN TO BRIDE AND GROOM] To both of you I wish you a long and happy journey!

CHAPTER 10:

Alternative Speakers

OVERVIEW

An alternative or proxy speaker is needed when the original person is unable to attend the wedding and deliver their speech. There are various reasons a speech role would need to be filled by a proxy or alternative speaker. The original, intended person may:

- have been called away for serious/private reasons (including illness)

- not be attending the wedding due to personal reasons

- have passed away recently.

Filling in for a person called away for serious/private reasons

If this occurs, it usually does so very close to the wedding day. It could be because of business or illness but, if you are the one filling in, you're probably panicking about the speech. Well don't. There are two ways you can get through this.

Firstly, before the original person has to fly (or whatever the case may be), get a hold of them. They may already have completed their speech, which could make your life a bit easier. In that case, you could simply give a short introduction briefly explaining why the original speaker was unable to attend, then read their speech. This depends on the sensitivity of the person's absence and if you do mention it, be diplomatic and smooth it over with some humor. If you wanted to, you could even modify their speech so that it comes from you. After all, you may have been requested to jump in by the wedding couple because you were the perfect choice.

Alternatively, you may wish to write your own speech from scratch. This all depends on the time remaining before the wedding. If there are a couple of days left, you should be able to drum something up. (Make sure you also run through the general speech writing instructions in Part II.) Depending on the role you've been asked to fill, base your speech on that particular speech role's chapter.

Finally, don't forget to include an apology from the original speaker. If their absence is due to illness, add in your wishes for a speedy recovery.

Filling in for someone who won't be attending due to personal reasons

When this occurs, it normally involves family members who may not be attending for historic family reasons. If you are filling in for this person, base your speech on the chapter covering the speech role they would be expected to perform.

As this is a sensitive subject (especially on a wedding day), it's obviously better not to discuss the reasons for the person's absence in your speech—only add that you were honored to be asked to perform this role. As for the role itself, alter any specific elements to reflect your relationship with the bride and groom. Finally, don't forget to include an apology from the original speaker.

Filling in for a person who has passed away

How you approach your speech depends on how long ago that person passed away (the speech will be especially sensitive if it occurred very recently). However, it is not as difficult a task as it might seem—you'll be basing your speech on that particular speech role's chapter. Alter the contents and tone of the speech to reflect what you want to say (based on your relationship with the bride and/or groom).

For more information see 'Discussing family or friends who have passed away' at the beginning of Part II.

Part II:

Plan, Write and Rehearse the Speech

♥♥♥♥♥♥♥♥♥ ♥ ♥♥♥♥♥♥♥♥♥

In Part II you'll learn how to plan and prepare what you want to say in your speech (Chapter 11). Once that's sorted, the next task is creating an outline of your speech (Chapter 12). The outline is a way of organising what you want to say, in the order you want to say it. The idea is to give you a structure to write your speech from.

With the outline complete, you'll be ready to write. Chapter 13 will guide you through the writing process, providing you with well-tested techniques and tips. Once your speech script is complete, you'll then find out about summarising and transferring it to a cue card—the cue card you'll be using on the day.

CHAPTER II:

Planning and Preparation

You've already begun your planning and preparation by reviewing the details of your speech role in Part I. The rest of the process will involve deciding what you want to say by choosing the memories and personal words you want to include, and creating a speech outline.

SPEECH-WRITING ELEMENTS TO KEEP IN MIND

Before you start, there are a number of aspects of speech-giving to keep in mind.

Order of speeches

Speeches were originally a short simple toast of 'to the bride and groom'. This toast eventually grew into 'a few words' and finally a full speech where the speakers offered their best wishes to the newly married couple. The traditional order of speeches has remained (that is, the father of the bride, the groom and the best man, in that order). Each speech role had a specific purpose.

To give you an idea of the speeches and the order you're most likely to encounter, the traditional sequence goes like this:

- father of the bride: opening speech, closing with the proposal of a toast to the bride and groom

- groom: response to the toast, speech and proposal of a second toast to the bridesmaids (on behalf of both himself and his new wife)

- best man: response to the toast and speech (on behalf of both himself and the bridesmaids).

The wedding couple should arrange the order of the speeches well in advance. The main reason, from a speechwriter's perspective, is to find out who comes before you and who will be introducing whom. Of course you can always make an adjustment, but that's not exactly what you want to be doing at the last minute, is it?

Today, the sequence (and number) of speeches varies. This is something for the wedding couple to decide on as part of their planning. You can never go wrong sticking with the traditional model. If more people will be speaking, it's usually better to include them after the best man.

There are a few last pieces of advice about planning the order of speeches:

- Always hold speeches *after* the wedding meal is finished, when energy levels are highest—speeches given to an audience on an empty stomach are a no-no. The guests (and the wedding party) have been on the go for hours and once they've eaten, they're ready to sit back, relax and listen.

- Don't get carried away and have too many people making speeches—it will dull the guests.

- The more speeches you have, the shorter each speech should be to balance the overall duration (except for the three traditional speakers).

- If at all possible, avoid sudden last minute requests by people wanting to make a speech—the thing you're trying to avoid is the ad lib speaker. An exception could be if the married couple are happy to let them speak and that person has prepared something.

- It's a good idea to have an MC manage the order of speeches and introduce the next speaker.

Deciding the length of the speech

Although there is no golden rule for a speech's duration, less is often more. Three to four minutes is considered the norm and some people even prefer very short speeches, which are essentially stretched out toasts that last about one minute.

Don't allow your speech to ramble, and shy away from complicated anecdotes. Still, speech length really depends on how the reception is planned and you should discuss this with the other speakers and the wedding couple.

Ethnic and cultural considerations

Today there are many marriages between couples from diverse cultural and ethnic backgrounds. This is an important consideration when writing a speech. The same goes for deciding the order of speeches.

If the married couple come from different ethnic backgrounds, ask if their culture has any particular marriage customs for speeches. For example, some European cultures traditionally have the father of the groom speak before the father of the bride.

The rule is to ask. Not only is this extra cultural consideration polite, it could also have a profoundly positive effect on the family and guests assembled.

Discussing family or friends who have passed away

Wedding speeches are a way of celebrating the day itself. That's why many people find it difficult or awkward to mention in their speech a close friend or family member who has passed away. This is completely understandable and the choice is entirely yours.

If on this very special day you wish to remember someone you have lost, there is nothing wrong with doing so. The general rule is simply to be tactful, respectful, and above all, human. It's a delicate matter, but handled gently it allows you to include the memory of this person in the day. It can be a very touching, kind and respectful inclusion—especially if that person would have been a close and important guest if they were with you all on the day.

Of course, much depends on the circumstances and the sensitivities of others present (and your personal beliefs). That's why it is a good idea to discuss this subject with those closest to the person concerned first. If you decide to go ahead, keep these aspects in mind:

- speak about the person as you would have spoken about them when they were alive

- depending on how well you knew the person (and if you're comfortable with it) comment on what they may have said on the day

- don't be afraid to be humorous when recalling them—especially if the person was a really funny character

- don't dwell on their loss, cherish the fact you knew them

- be wary of your words upsetting anyone or diminishing the general mood of a day set aside for celebration

- be aware of causing any cultural or religious offence—in some cultures, discussing such matters at a wedding is considered disrespectful, painful or incredibly poor etiquette.

Once you've finished speaking of the person, it's important to bring the guests back to the moment and the celebration. This is not discourteous; it ensures that the celebratory mood is not affected.

If the bride and/or groom have previously been married

If the bride and groom have been married before, you may feel uncomfortable saying anything about that marriage. The general rule is to avoid mentioning previous relationships anyway and the same goes for previous marriages. For some, mentioning a previous marriage may cause offence and even detract from the uniqueness of the day for the wedding couple. Today is theirs and the past is in the past.

If there are children present from a previous marriage or relationship

If the bride or groom has children present from a previous relationship or marriage it's obviously important not to hurt any child's feelings. It all boils down to the circumstances and the people involved.

The best advice is still not to mention the ex-partner (the child's biological father or mother). However, do make sure the children are mentioned. This is especially the case in the groom's (and/or bride's) wedding speech. In their case, it's vital to make the child feel welcomed and included.

Consider the age of the child and how they may perceive your words. If both the bride and groom have children from a previous marriage, ensure mention of them is balanced. Children can be eerily aware of favouritism. Remember: the wedding means the beginning of a new life for children in such circumstances too.

Liaise with the wedding party

Before writing, it's a good idea to find out in what order the speeches will be given. The wedding couple may also have a set idea about how long they want the speeches to be. Some weddings have more speakers than others, which will affect your speech's duration and content.

Always keep your audience in mind

Although you're addressing your speech to specific people on the wedding day, you need to keep all of the wedding guests in mind. It may seem obvious but it's actually one of the biggest flaws in wedding speeches.

For example, if you recall a funny event which is an in-joke amongst only a couple of the guests, the rest of the audience may feel left out. Not only will you (and your in-joke group) be laughing alone, you may also have alienated the audience.

Use the opportunity to be as open as you wish

Your speech is a rare chance, when you have the undivided attention of your friends and relatives, to tell your loved ones how you honestly feel about them: how much you love them and what they mean to you.

I recall one father of the bride who had always felt awkward and shy about publicly expressing his feelings for his daughter (you know, the only cry when cutting onions man). In his speech he put his heart on his sleeve like he'd never done before. There weren't any onions at the reception, but there sure were a lot of wet eyes and touched smiles. For him and his daughter, it was one of the most special moments they had shared. So make the most of it. Of course, don't get too emotional—after all, you don't want to turn it into a wailing session or turn yourself into a blubbering mess and get helped off the stage like James Brown.

DECIDE WHAT YOU WANT YOUR SPEECH TO SAY

Other than the details you've already identified in Part I, you will need brief lists of items such as stories or anecdotes about the bride or groom and what they mean to you. You'll be using these stories to create the core of your speech—the parts that bring a loving or laughing tear to the eyes of the guests.

So let's get cracking. You'll need a notepad, pencil and eraser (erasing mistakes will make your notes easier to read). You'll also need peace and quiet. Yes, that means turn the TV off and lock yourself away somewhere relaxing and quiet. Wherever—as long as you won't be disturbed every few minutes. If anybody complains, just wave this book at them in explanation and make growling noises!

There are three main elements in wedding speeches. How much of each element you use is up to you because you're the one who is going to be writing and delivering the speech. The three elements of a speech we'll go through are:

- standard and traditional items for your role on the day (already identified in Part I)

- poignant, humorous or significant anecdotes, stories or memories

- how you feel about the people you are writing about.

Remember: you only have a couple of minutes to speak on the day. When you're preparing the speech outline, you'll only be selecting a handful of items from the lists to include in the speech, so don't get too carried away writing pages and pages. Your speech shouldn't be long enough to be available in leading bookshops! Try to keep your lists relatively short.

Standard and traditional content

On the top of your new page write the heading 'TRADITIONAL THINGS IN MY SPEECH' in block capitals.

You have already found out in Part I how your role's speech is traditionally structured, along with its contents. (If you haven't, go through it now.) As mentioned in Part I, you can decide how much you want to stick to traditional elements in your speech. These days, wedding speeches are far more flexible and personal—it's all up to you. From your speech role (in Part I) copy down the speech contents you want to use or have been asked to use in your speech. Once you're finished, pull out that page.

Anecdotes, stories and memories

On the top of your new blank page, write the heading 'STORIES' in block capitals. Relax. Clear your mind.

Picture the people your speech will be about. Picture them as you normally see them. Think back as long as they've been in your life and replay memories you have of them. Some memories will obviously stand out above others.

On your notepad, write down the memories coming to you. It can be in single words, phrases or a couple of sentences recalling special, humorous or important events in the bride or groom's life. Don't worry about exact words or profound statements, just write them as they come. Leave a blank line between each memory on the page.

Write on only one side of the page and try to keep your list to one page. Remember to erase mistakes and not to scratch them out.

Neater notes make for easy referencing when you're creating your outline later on.

To help trigger some memories, have a look through the following words and phrases:

- birth
- school
- sports
- painting
- animals
- work
- backyard

- birthdays
- meeting for the first time
- first car
- dates
- parties
- holiday trips and travel

A great way of getting the full picture of an event is to have a word with friends or family members. They'll either add an extra angle to the story or maybe even prompt another one. Don't get too carried away—relating memories in a speech can occupy a large amount of your speaking time. It's recommended that you distil your list down to one or two of the 'best' memories.

How do you know which are the best stories for your speech? Avoid ones requiring a lot of explanation. It's your choice, but there are two types of memories that work well in wedding speeches:

- events illustrating to the guests the character, qualities and life of those you're speaking about
- events illustrating your feelings for them or your relationship.

You may even find that certain memories sum up both of the above. Use the ones that work best for you. Once you're finished, pull out that page.

How you feel about them

On the top of your new page write the heading 'HOW I FEEL ABOUT THEM' in block capitals.

Picture yourself at the coming wedding. Picture the people you're going to be speaking about. Erase any images of chatting guests, sounds or laughter. You're happily alone with the people you'll be speaking about and to, no-one else.

What do they mean to you? What do you want to say to them on this important day in their lives?

On your notepad, write down what pops into your head about how you feel. Again, it can be in single words, phrases or a couple of sentences expressing how you have felt about them for as long as you've known them and especially how you feel about them on their big day. Don't worry about exact words or profound statements. Leave a blank line between each thought.

Now that this list is complete, re-read it and pull it out of the notepad, putting it aside.

CHAPTER 12:

Creating the Outline of the Speech

Now that you have at least three pages of lists, creating the outline structure is straightforward enough:

- lay down the traditional structure (as you've modified it to your requirements)

- figure out where each of the memories you've chosen will go in the outline

- blend in how you feel about the people you are writing about.

LAY DOWN THE BASE STRUCTURE

The best place to start is using the traditional elements for your role (i.e. the list headed 'Traditional things in my speech'). Feel free to try various versions of the outline until you're happy it covers what you want to say.

- On a new blank page, write the heading 'OUTLINE'

- draw a line down the left side of the page and mark a bullet point at the top of the line and write out the first item from your 'Traditional things in my speech' list (you should have already sorted out the order you want to use)

- leave a gap of two blank lines below the first one, mark another bullet and write out the second item from the list and so on

- once that's done, you'll be looking at the basic outline of your speech.

Now it's time to add the spice.

ADD YOUR ANECDOTES

- Look at the speech outline—you should have one or two spots for stories/memories

- refer to your 'Memories' list and copy the anecdotes or memories that you have chosen into the speech outline

- look at the outline and consider where you'd like to include your points touching on how you feel about them—you'll probably find this section works better when blended into your anecdotes or throughout your written speech script.

Review the speech outline

Time to relax and clear your mind again. Take your time and read through the outline. Think about how it feels. Are you happy with the flow of it? Don't worry too much about how it sounds yet—leave that for the writing stage. Move things around if you want.

Remember: you don't have to stick to the traditional structure if you don't want to. The only elements that shouldn't really change are the toasts and the thankyous.

CHAPTER 13:

Writing the Speech

Now that you have completed the speech outline, you have a good structure to start writing from. Before you start, I have news for you: this part is far easier than you may think.

By the end of this chapter, you will have a completed speech script. We'll get there by using the speech outline as the scaffolding to build around. This chapter will explain:

- ten golden rules of speech writing

- writing the speech—the process

- starting the speech—hooking the audience from the first line

- language—drawing in the audience with rhythm, pace, flow etc.

- using humor

- using quotations (from poetry, proverbs, famous people etc.)

- deciding the length of the speech

- using symbolism and creating pictures

- being expressive and poignant

- closing the speech.

THE GOLDEN RULES OF WRITING A WEDDING SPEECH

Behind every speech there are golden rules that have helped many a speechwriter hold it together well. These golden rules can be referred to at any time while you're writing. Some are common sense, the rest are dealt with in detail in this section.

1   Write in your natural voice. You are speaking to those who know you and hearing a familiar voice at a wedding, speaking openly and honestly about their loved ones, is naturally eloquent and touching.

2   Write from the heart and give your words due meaning.

3   Write it as it is—shy away from romanticising the couple or their past, be honest while being discreet.

4   Don't be afraid to say emotional and poignant things it's a wedding and you're allowed to.

5   Throw in some humor.

6   Write as much as you need to (time permitting) and make every word count. I know you could just keep on going, but remember you've only got a few minutes.

7   Avoid repetition and don't repeat subjects … because repetition is bad … and repetitive.

8   The best speeches inform and involve an audience.

9 Remember to follow your speech outline.

10 Don't offend your audience (especially the wedding couple!).

HOW YOU'LL BE WRITING THE SPEECH: FROM OUTLINE TO SCRIPT TO CUE CARD

To create the final speech you will write the script from the speech outline and then reduce the script to a cue card.

A script is actually the proper name for a speech written out word for word as you will be saying it on the night. A cue card is that very same script, only reduced to point form. The reason you shouldn't simply read from the entire script on the night is straightforward.

Picture this: a speaker steps up to the microphone and for four minutes reads from a prepared speech without raising their eyes from the page. By the end, half of the room looks like they've been drugged and the other half looks like they wish they were.

You've probably experienced this. The speech sounds monotonous because the speaker is purely concentrating on reading the words— they fail to engage the audience's interest. Reading straight from a script can strip words of all naturalness and spontaneity. The last thing you want is to sound as if you are reading from a prepared speech (yes, the irony). That's why rehearsing the speech using cue cards (to be used on the night) results in a better sounding and presented speech.

Before you start the first line, you'll need to familiarise yourself with the rules of writing a speech. By the end of this chapter, you'll be wondering what all the worry was about in the first place.

STARTING THE SPEECH: HOOKING THE AUDIENCE FROM THE FIRST LINE

Ah, the first line. Your first line is what professional writers of all varieties call 'the hook'. Your first line has to capture the audience's attention and get them immediately interested. It's then a case of keeping them interested and closing the speech tidily.

Now, back to the first line and the hook. This is your opening comment and statement and there are various types of hooks you could use:

- a famous and/or literary quotation

- humor

- anniversary links to the day

- bracketing the first and last lines of the speech.

A famous/literary quotation

Quotations can come from writers, philosophers, lovers, or all three. In a wedding speech, the quotations you use should relate to love, marriage, friendship or family. Has anyone ever said something profound or touching to you about these subjects? Maybe you know of a line from a book, film or poem?

The wonderful thing about humanity is that we've written vast amounts on love. This isn't surprising, as love is the steady star we sail our lives by (you can quote me on that!). You'll find many sources for quotations—pop into a bookshop or library and you'll find such quotations in the reference and poetry sections.

When you've found a quotation, blend it into the first point of your speech. Don't waste words explaining the background of the quotation (the writer or the book etc.). The opening line must be clear and catchy. This is the first line, so you can't afford to throw in extra information that will detract from the meaning and message of the quotation.

Here are a few examples of opening lines using quotations.

Ladies and gentlemen, a man once wrote, 'Love creates a past which envelops us, as if by enchantment.' Today we come together to celebrate and witness that very same enchantment gently envelop [BRIDE] and [GROOM] in marriage. [PAUSE] I believe love hasn't only created their past—it has created a beautiful future together for them …

Ladies and gentlemen, it is said, 'Absence sharpens love, [PAUSE] presence strengthens it.' [PAUSE] Seeing [BRIDE] and [GROOM] earlier today and here now provides the best example of love's strength one could ever hope to see …

Ladies and gentlemen, E M Forster once said, 'Love is a great force in life, it is indeed the greatest of all things.' I couldn't agree more with him after having the honor of witnessing the marriage today of [BRIDE] and [GROOM].

Ladies and gentlemen, we are born seeking love. [PAUSE] Well, Oscar Wilde advised us, 'When you really want love, you will find it waiting for you.' And I believe [BRIDE] and [GROOM] did find it waiting for them—there in each other, [PAUSE] at the ceremony today and here, right at this moment.

You could even open with a poem. This is especially poignant in a groom's speech (or a bride's). The best advice if using a poem is to choose a very short one or use the most striking verse. It allows you to start the speech in a less traditional way. Here's an example:

'She is the promise/given by the stroke/of a calming breeze/in hills bath'd by love's first sunrise.' Ladies and gentlemen, a sunrise brings hope, beauty and promise. Tomorrow will be our first sunrise together as husband and wife. [PAUSE] The sun first rose for me the moment [BRIDE] and I met.

Poetry is used more and more these days, but use it only if you feel comfortable with it and it connects with how you feel.

Bracketing the speech

Bracketing is where the first lines connect with the last lines of your speech, bringing it full circle. It's a case of set-up and pay-off. You'll get the idea in the following example.

First lines (the set-up): Ladies and gentlemen, when [BRIDE] was five years old she asked me what makes the sun shine. She asked dozens of those questions day after day. [YOUR WIFE] and I gave the best answers we could, but she sometimes looked back at us as if we were a little slow in the head. [PAUSE FOR LAUGHTER] But, as she grew up, [BRIDE] became the one with the answers, while we asked the questions.

Finally, just a year ago, [GROOM] asked her a real cracker of a question. [PAUSE] And wouldn't you know it— she had the answer! [PAUSE FOR LAUGHTER] Well, I'm proud and happy to say that is why we're here today …

Last lines of the same speech (the pay-off): After all of the planning they put into today, I'm not surprised it went wonderfully smoothly, as it has. It seemed like everything happened on cue—the ceremony, the seating—even the sun seemed to work to schedule. [PAUSE] Which reminds me, [BRIDE] all those years ago, I don't think I answered your question about what makes the sun shine. [PAUSE] Well, seeing you and [GROOM] together today, I think the answer speaks for itself.

Then the toast would be proposed. Bracketing can be difficult, but if you get it working it's a real winner.

LANGUAGE: DRAWING IN THE AUDIENCE

The words you write need to be able to translate into natural and comfortable sounds. As I said earlier, when you're delivering your speech you have to sound like you're not reading from one at all.

Don't forget, most people at the wedding will know you well enough to know your style of speaking. The human voice has a variety of qualities, making each one distinctive. You may have heard of security devices that can tell the identity of a person based on their 'voiceprint'. Just like a fingerprint, each of us has a different voice—deep or high, singsong or flat, gravelly or smooth. On top of that we have our own unique way of phrasing our words.

As most of the wedding guests will be familiar with your particular way of speaking, this allows you to, well … be yourself! It also makes writing your speech script a thousand times easier than writing a formal speech. If your speech is formal, you won't connect with the audience. That connection is crucial to how your words are received (their effect) and how you handle yourself throughout the speech (e.g. nerves).

To give you a better, more in-depth understanding of this we'll look at the main elements of language that you need to be aware of in a speech including:

- formal versus natural voice

- pace

- rhythm

- flow

- crafting words using images and symbolism.

Formal versus natural voice

Ask most people to write a few words to say in public and they may write what is called text. A 'text' is written to be read, not said. It's formal and generally obeys grammatical rules. To give you an idea, read this aloud: 'A wedding day is not only a ceremony. A wedding day is a celebration.'

Great at school, not in a speech to loved ones. So, what you'll be writing is a 'script'. The same text would sound much better like this (read it aloud): 'A wedding day isn't just a ceremony—it's a celebration.'

The script will capture your normal manner of speaking and people will warm to your words more. You'll also find it much easier to rehearse your speech when its language is your language.

Pace

Although the words will be written in the same way you speak, you still must alter them to give the audience a chance to absorb certain points and to become involved in your story. Your speech is not simply a task of uttering words—it's sharing wishes, feelings and memories with the wedding party and guests. Just imagine you are in the audience listening to your speech (this technique is discussed further on). Does it draw you in? Does it interest you? The best speeches inform and involve the audience.

Write your sentences to match your voice and your breathing pattern. Go over it and see where you need to pause to allow the audience to absorb a point or draw them into one. Pauses are also very effective in the gap between a question you ask, and the answer you give.

You can insert pauses in different formats—use what appeals to you. Have a look at this example of pauses in use.

When [BRIDE] and [GROOM] told us they were going to marry I thought ahead and wondered how I'd feel on the wedding day. [PAUSE] Is our little girl leaving us? Will she stop helping me with my tax returns? Will we still be father and daughter? [PAUSE] Well, when she placed her arm in mine today all I could feel was immense pride and complete love for our little girl, for this beautiful woman ... our daughter and now also [GROOM'S] wonderful wife.

Rhythm

Another technique to help draw in the audience is rhythm. This is the use and placement of certain words to create a natural feeling of rhythm. If you've read or heard poetry or fiction, then you'll have encountered rhythm. There are two very effective types of rhythm you can use: alliteration and parallel sentences.

Alliteration is the recurrence of sounds (and syllables). This is normally done with the beginning of words. For example, 'May you always have love and laughter in your life.'

The alliteration here was the recurrence of the letter 'l' in 'love', 'laughter' and 'life'. This technique adds lyrical rhythm to such a simple phrase. Use it sparingly, and most of all, use it where it counts. The above example was used to express the speaker's wishes for the married couple.

You'll also find alliteration works best in a series of three (as in the above example). Don't get carried away with it or you may find yourself getting tongue-tied.

Parallel sentences can be used to stress a point or a series of points. For example, 'Love makes the impossible possible … Love warms us on cold days … Love gives us something to live for … Love is pure … Love is what I see tonight between [BRIDE] and [GROOM].'

As you can see, parallel sentences used in this way allow you to put something such as the love between people in a grander context. It also allows you to phrase what you want to say in a neat and clear manner.

Flow

Flow is ensuring a smooth connection from one point to another. If you've ever tried explaining to a person how to do a certain task you would have used flow: 'You close the door. *Then* you turn the dial all the way to the right.'

Then was used to keep the flow and clarify the next point.

In a speech, it's not too hard to write a couple of sentences to cover a certain point. However, most people find it difficult to keep the flow of their speech going. You can also create flow through a rhetorical question:

What kept me going despite all this? [PAUSE] [BRIDE]. She never let me give up on myself.

In the next example, the word 'meanwhile' is used to bridge two connected points.

I spent weeks wondering if [BRIDE] was even remotely interested in me. I didn't want to look a fool and ask, but I didn't want to lose her either ... *meanwhile*, it turns out she was prying information from my friends to find out if I was interested in her!

It may seem obvious, but many people neglect the flow of their speech. It's a valuable way of keeping the audience's attention and there are many words and phrases you can use to improve the flow, including *however, anyway, anyhow, at the same time.*

You'll find the ones which work for you when you start re-reading your script out loud. That's also when you'll spot where there are problems with flow in the first place. How? Well, whenever a piece in your speech seems disjointed or too sudden or out of place—that's a flow problem. Try different ways of saying it aloud and connecting to the next point. Sometimes that next point just may not fit.

Crafting words: using images and symbolism

To add life to words in your speech, try out techniques used by writers (especially fiction writers). These are especially effective when used in any stories or anecdotes you may be including.

For example, say you had a line like this:

Then one day, we went for a drive in the country. We stopped at a lake and I got down on one knee and asked her if she would marry me.

That same line could be re-written as:

One bright January morning, I sprung the idea on [BRIDE] to take a drive into the country … to see where the road took us. Of course, I already had a place in mind—a small sparkling lake surrounded by grassy rolling hills. [PAUSE] It was there we stopped. We walked down to the edge of the water. After a moment, I knelt on one knee, looked up at her and asked if she'd be my wife.

Now, although that stretched the length out somewhat, it was worth it for such an important part of the speech. Sure, you need to watch quantity, but don't concentrate on that at the cost of quality.

Of course, sometimes it takes fewer words to better describe an image. Instead of saying, 'She looked at me and started smiling and crying and nodding.' Try saying, 'Her eyes gave me her answer.'

Figurative language is another way of describing something in a more interesting way—similes and metaphors give language an extra angle. A simile is where you compare one thing to another. The two are usually linked by using 'as' or 'like'. For example, 'As happy *as* a cat with cream.' Or, 'It flew *like* an oil tanker.'

So, instead of, 'We laughed all evening.' Try, 'We laughed *like lunatics* all evening.'

A metaphor is different—it transforms one thing to another. For example:

> I knew [BRIDE] was planning a trip somewhere even though she denied it. My suspicions were realised two days later when I opened the cleaning closet and was attacked by flocks of travel brochures, tumbling and plunging out of their hidden nest.

Obviously travel brochures are not grouped together as 'flocks'. But it adds to the imagery as did the use of 'tumbling and plunging'.

So, where you can, or where the speech needs it, spice it up. Don't get too carried away with every sentence, just use it here or there. Try to get the audience to visualise what you're describing—it'll make your story richer and draw them in.

Using humor

Humor is a great way to break the ice and open a speech. A wedding is a celebration after all and opening with humor is the best technique for relaxing people and encouraging them to enjoy the event. It could be a joke or a witty anecdote. However, humor in a wedding speech must also be used carefully.

A witty anecdote (which you may have identified in the planning stage earlier) is always a welcome inclusion in a wedding speech. It could be a funny story about either the bride or groom. Maybe about when they were a child. Perhaps in the lead-up to the wedding day there was a goof up, which now, in the safety of the past, is worth telling. Whatever you choose, just be sure it won't cause offence and doesn't require a laborious explanation. Remember: the hook has to catch the audience.

The same goes for straightforward jokes. There is a very fine line between having them rolling in the aisles and having them rolling their eyes in polite pain. Remember: you are writing for the audience.

The saying goes in comedy: if in doubt, leave it out. The general rules for jokes or humor are:

- Are you comfortable enough to be able to tell the joke properly?

- Will the joke be well received and understood by nearly all of the audience? The guests could range from toddlers to a hundred years old.

- eave in-jokes out unless you can adequately let the audience in on the joke beforehand. Family or groups of friends may have a running joke—fine, but will it be lost on the rest of the audience?

- Obviously, sexist, racist, ageist or any form of minority jokes may result in hurt feelings (theirs or yours) or hurt noses (yours).

- The same applies for dirty jokes or risqué comments— risqué is generally fine, up to a point.

- Steer clear of making harsh jokes about the married couple—especially the bride. If you are absolutely positive they won't be offended make sure you close up the joke with serious praise (but, watch this one—it has gone wrong at many a wedding).

Using props

Props or other stage equipment (excluding rubber chickens!) are a great way of enhancing a joke or funny story. They are also a handy technique for making the other guests feel included in the event.

Props can be used as physical gags in themselves (e.g. a book presented as marital advice such as *War and Peace* or *Cooking for Dummies*). Props are also useful for illustrating a funny story. For example, while recalling what the groom was like as a child you may have some of his toys (teddy bear, toy car, action figure). To really push it you could invent the truth and announce his mother gave you some of his childhood toys to show at the reception and then produce a Barbie doll.

Another gag is to read from a fake letter supposedly written by either the bride or groom as a child. Write in a childish language, but have it come across as slightly adult-level. It could be about anything—make them out to be a monster, an evil scientist or just plain nuts—whatever you think the guests might briefly find believable. Of course, don't tell them it's a fake until the end (or maybe not at all—keep them guessing).

CLOSING THE SPEECH

What impression would you like to leave the audience with at the end of your speech? Whatever it is, that will guide you for your closing lines. Similar to the opening lines, it could be humorous or sentimental.

Your speech should flow to a neat close and not leave the audience hanging in the air. Depending on your role on the day, once your core speech has ended the only item left will be your particular role's toast proposal. For examples, refer to the sample speeches in Part I.

TRANSFERRING FROM A SCRIPT TO A CUE CARD

The idea of a cue card is to summarise the main topics of your speech in point form and in sequence.

When you finalise your speech in full script form (i.e. word for word) you'll have to practice it (covered later in Part III). Don't panic—you won't believe how easy it actually is to get your script practiced enough to allow you to read from a cue card on the night.

For a cue card you can use a single (or more) standard-sized summary card (also known as index cards), which you'll find in most stationery shops. Otherwise, you can simply use a sheet of paper.

To transfer your completed script to a cue card, review the script and write down its main topics in short, single lines. Write it out roughly until you're happy that each line captures what you want to say on each topic. These 'one-liner' points can even be the first sentence of each topic—use whatever jogs your memory the best.

Later, when you are practising, you may find that some topics in your speech need prompting on the cue card more than others, so adjust the cue card to match.

Cue card example

Write out the words in large clear capital letters, making the card easier to read. The example below is short, but you can put more on your cards, if it helps. You may find you want to note down some specific phrases, quotations or details. Just remember to keep the lines short and write out only enough to prompt your memory.

By the time you've practiced your speech enough, the cue card will only serve as a prompt. Some people find they don't use it in the end, but it helps to create one anyway.

Here's a short example of a father of the bride's cue card:

1   BEFORE I START, I'D LIKE TO THANK:

   • [GROOM'S] PARENTS FOR THEIR HELP

   • GUESTS FOR COMING

2   QUOTE FROM POEM

3   STORY: DAY [BRIDE] BROUGHT [GROOM] HOME

4   WISHES FOR THEIR FUTURE

5   TOAST TO BRIDE AND GROOM

Part III:

Delivering Your Speech—a Survival Guide

❤❤❤❤❤❤❤❤ ❤ ❤❤❤❤❤❤❤❤

You've completed your speech script and transferred it to cue cards. Your speech is ready—the only thing left is getting *you* ready.

The big fear people have about speeches is not the writing part—the big fear is finally delivering it on the day. Well, by the end of this book we'll try to turn that big fear into a tiny fear.

Why would a person not look forward to delivering a speech to a room full of people?

Answer: The idea of delivering a speech to a room full of people is a little unnerving. Why is it unnerving? Answer: I'm not really sure I can stand up there and confidently deliver a speech. I'm worried I might screw up or people will see just how nervous I am. It's not like I make speeches every day, you know.

And that's the key. The underlying problem for nearly everyone is that because they don't give speeches regularly, they don't feel confident that they can deliver their speech well enough. That's perfectly normal. So, how can you try to get past this? Well, what if you:

- learn how to use your voice effectively?

- learn how to hold your posture correctly?

- practice your speech enough that the words came easily?

- learn how to minimise your nerves?

This section will guide you through these techniques so you'll be in a much better position to step up, cope with any nerves and deliver your speech successfully.

CHAPTER 14:

Using Your Voice Effectively

The way you use your voice in normal everyday conversation is very different from the way you use it to address a room full of people. In public speaking, you are using your voice to paint a picture in the minds of the audience.

Remember: the rule of a good speech is to get the audience's attention, say what you want to say, and leave them feeling happy.

Try to make your tone of voice colorful. Think how you would describe a walk through a forest to someone without sight—your choice of words and emphasis would have to change dramatically.

Also, regardless of whether you have the use of a microphone or not, your words will need to be heard clearly. People won't hear you if you speak too fast, too quietly or squeeze the entire speech in one tense breath. So, how do you ensure your words will be heard—and clearly? In this chapter, you'll learn a few aspects of voice usage in public speaking such as:

- assessing your voice

- emphasizing and clearly pronouncing words

- pacing your words

- microphone or no microphone?

ASSESS YOUR VOICE

First of all, you need to find out what elements of your public speaking voice will need attention, so, it's a good idea if you take a little time-out to assess your voice. Get hold of a tape recorder (or other recording device) for this. (If you can't get a recording device, ask someone to help listen to you test-read your speech. Have that person sit away from you, preferably in a large room.)

Read your speech out loud and record it. Give it a couple of tries if you like. When you're finished, play it back and see how clearly you've spoken. Try to listen to it as if you are a guest. Your speech should be clear to basically everybody at the reception. This is what you are listening out for:

- did you sound too flat or monotonous and like you were concentrating too much?

- did you make good uses of pauses to add expectation or let a point sink in?

- did you emphasize certain phrases or words sufficiently in order to hammer home a particular point?

- did you speak too fast or too slow?

- did you speak clearly enough to identify every word easily?

- is the message you want to convey getting across?

Voice tone and pitch

When you're comfortable and speaking in normal conversation, the tone of your voice will vary depending on what you're speaking about, to whom and whether it's light-hearted or serious. The pitch of your voice also changes to match these criteria. However, when it comes to public speaking, people tend to be distracted by their nervousness and as a result they end up speaking in a monotone and raising the pitch of their voice.

There is no perfect tone or pitch in speech delivery. The perfect tone and pitch are those which best suit your own voice and the speech you are giving. Listen to the recording of your speech and identify where you could alter the tone and pitch to emphasize certain areas.

It's important to keep the audience listening. This can be achieved through changing your emphasis in tone and pitch. Newsreaders on TV and radio use such changes to capture and keep your attention.

Speaking of news, the good news is, the more you practice your speech before the wedding, the better you will know the right tone and pitch to use. As you get to know and be comfortable with the words, you'll have to concentrate less. And, as with normal conversation, your words will sound far more natural.

EMPHASIZING WITH WORDS AND WITHOUT WORDS
Emphasizing with words

Listening to your speech played back, you may already have spotted where some words required more emphasis than others.

For example, instead of, '… that's when I knew she was serious', add emphasis to the most important word in the sentence—the one at the heart of what you're trying to say in any particular sentence or paragraph.

So, the above example may end up, '… that's when I *knew* she was serious.'

Not only does this technique emphasize certain core elements of your speech, but it also guides guests and keeps their attention.

Emphasizing without words

Although pauses were discussed in Part II of this book, now that you are polishing the sound of the speech and are increasingly familiar with your written words, you may spot areas of your speech requiring better placement of pauses. This may be because a certain point needs to be allowed to sink in. This is especially effective in serious and poignant parts of a speech—a well-placed pause adds to the feeling of importance and sincerity.

Pauses also create a gap between one point and the next point. If you're telling a funny story or a joke, a pause will create that air of anticipation required to deliver a punchline. If you are changing from one subject to another (and therefore changing from one tone to another) a pause will allow you to do this without causing confusion.

Don't overuse pauses or your speech may come across with too many gaps and silences but if there is a pause (comma, full stop or your own inserted [PAUSE]) in your speech then obey it. If you don't, you might confuse or lose the audience (or yourself). Remember: if you have a pause between a touching or sentimental subject and a new or up-beat subject, make sure you invigorate the audience as you move out of the pause by using the most fitting tone to best match each section of the speech. It's a ride—take them on it.

GETTING THE POINT ACROSS CLEARLY

Beyond your voice's tone and pitch, your words need to be heard clearly. Other than how loud or soft you need to speak (discussed later), you need to make sure you're not speaking too fast and that your words are coming across clearly.

Pace (or speed)

Listen to your recording. Are you rushing through your words? Be wary of this especially on the night as nerves can cause people to race through their speech. (It's as if they want to get the whole thing over with or something! Imagine!)

It may seem appealing to rush, but don't do it. If you rush, you're more likely to make a mistake. Also, guests will not be given the chance to absorb key points—in the end, you'll have finished your speech in record time, but no-one will have really got into it.

So, set the pace of your speech to suit your style. On the night, your breathing will probably be faster (due to some nerves). If you can, practice your speech at a pace that is easy to you, it should also help lessen the nerves on the night. By that stage you should find the pace occurs far more naturally (via repetition).

Of course, this doesn't mean you need to ... speak ... too ... slowly. Just make sure the pace doesn't slow down to the stage where people are falling asleep.

Articulation

While your speech is designed to sound natural when spoken in your voice, you need to make that sure each word can clearly be understood and distinguished from the other. Theatre actors, like public speakers, achieve this through articulation and projection.

PROJECTING YOUR VOICE: MICROPHONE OR NO MICROPHONE?

Do you know if the reception will have a microphone? Whether or not there is one affects how you project your voice.

With a microphone

The important thing to remember about microphones is that their sensitivity varies. Different PA (public address) systems and different locations produce different qualities of sound. On top of that, people sometimes find it difficult to gauge how loud or soft they should speak with a microphone. When we're up there, we tend to mainly hear the sound from our own mouth and not the PA system.

As a general rule, don't have the microphone too close to your mouth. This overloads the output making it difficult for guests to clearly discern your words (many of you will have heard this effect before). It's a good idea to find out if the venue has a microphone beforehand. The staff may also be familiar with the sound quality and levels, so you could discuss it with them.

However, if all else fails you can always adjust your voice when you step up. At the beginning of your speech, look towards the back of the room—are people straining to hear you? You may need to raise the level of your voice a little but you won't need to raise it too dramatically or shout. Remember to speak at a slow and steady pace, clearly pronouncing your words.

Just remember to relax before you first speak—take in a few slow, easy, steady breaths as you prepare yourself (more on preparation later).

Without a microphone

Articulation and projection really come into play if there is no microphone at the venue. Exaggerate your lip movements when pronouncing words. Speak firmly and confidently. One side effect of forcing yourself to 'speak to be heard' is it boosts your confidence. They say fear feeds itself—well confidence also feeds itself. If you make yourself sound confident, you'll begin to feel more confident.

The very best way of ensuring you'll be heard by everyone is to use another theatre technique. Pretend you are speaking directly to those furthest away from you. If there are people down the back, your voice should be loud and clear enough to be heard by them. Again, don't raise your voice to the point of shouting.

CHAPTER 15:

Body Language – Posture and Gesture

The way you hold your body in public speaking and the use of body language make a difference to the quality of your speech.

POSTURE

When a person is nervous, they tend to stand with their shoulders curled in and head down. This conveys the wrong message to the audience and restricts your ability to speak confidently and well. Nerves also cause a speaker's airway to tighten and this can hammer away at our confidence and voice control.

No-one expects a world-shaking orator—everyone expects and understands some degree of nervousness. However, if a speaker is hunched up with nerves, the audience will switch onto this and be drawn away from your words. This goes against a speaker's most important task—to draw in the crowd. Ah! But there is a solution!

What to do

To project a confident image remember to keep your:

- head upright
- shoulders relaxed
- back straight
- chest out.

Also, place your feet firmly on the ground about shoulder width apart. Other than projecting confident body language, this also frees up your air passage so you will be able to control and project your voice far better. People will react positively and as a result, you will too. So (literally), chin up!

What not to do

Body language is a funny thing. Often the way we hold ourselves can be misconstrued by those around us. When you're giving your speech:

- don't lean on the table or lectern—it conveys aggression while also making you tense up
- don't dig your hands into your pockets—again it will cause you to hunch and tense up and your hands will get sweaty, possibly triggering more nerves
- don't tense your legs—every now and then subtly shift your weight from one leg to the other (but don't get carried away looking like you need to bolt for the toilet)
- don't fold your arms in front of you—it conveys defensiveness.

Remember: you want to draw the audience in with your happiness and friendliness.

GESTURE

Gestures are the non-verbal words in your speech. Similar to a speaker's posture, there are some 'dos and don'ts'.

What to do

Use gestures to enhance certain elements of your speech. Gestures can be:

- hand movements
- facial expressions
- eye contact
- head movements.

Some people are known to talk with their hands. It's a very expressive method for conveying a story. Nerves have a habit of restricting hand movement, but once you start moving as you normally would in conversation, you'll find you relax more (your body will feel like it's in familiar territory).

Facial expressions are another natural communicator of feelings and ideas. Again, the more you allow your body to speak as it does in normal conversation, the more you'll relax. And what's one of the best facial expressions to use? Your natural smile.

Eye contact is another important element. Don't fix your eyes too long on one person or thing. Think of a fly-fisher constantly casting a lure onto the water. You can keep the audience's attention by regularly casting your eyes out to different parts of the room (along with moving your body). Of course, don't 'cast' too much or you'll get dizzy.

If something in your speech could do with a head movement, such as a puzzled tilt to the side, use it. This physical action not only enhances what you've just said, it acts as a trigger to the audience (again, drawing them in).

Finally, to get comfortable with your gestures for the night, include them with your speech practice. Do this in front of a long mirror or a video camera.

What not to do

Some people worry when they're up speaking that the audience will be watching their every move for a flaw. This isn't the case. Ask yourself, have you deliberately done this? No, most likely not. However, people will be aware if you get carried away and make too many forced gestures. So:

- don't add so many gestures that they become a distraction (both for yourself and your audience)

- don't clasp your hands together as you speak—you may begin tensing them which will then make you tense

- don't wag your finger or raise a clenched fist unless it's obviously humorous—as you can tell, it conveys threat

- don't allow your hands to play with your speech, your watch or your shirt collar (it's an obvious sign of nerves)

- don't lift your hand in front of your mouth as it will block the sound

- don't try to force your smile—if you're nervous or your smile muscles have had a work-out all day—and it could end up looking like a grimace.

CHAPTER 16:

Coping With Nerves

You'll be happy to know, now that you have those public speaking techniques under your belt and have begun practising your speech, you're already well prepared to cope with nerves on the night. Again, just like learning to ride a bicycle, once you have the basic training, the fear is already greatly reduced.

I say greatly reduced, because practically anyone delivering a speech in public gets nervous (before and during). It's completely natural. Nerves only become a problem in a speech if you're not confident reading your material or you don't calm yourself properly beforehand.

With the techniques you've learned so far and by practising your speech, the first cause is dealt with. In this chapter you'll learn to manage your nerves as well as how to deal with speech speed bumps such as mistakes and interruptions.

Believe it or not, the guests sitting out there are on your side. This is not a job interview or a courtroom plea for clemency. This is you speaking to people who, just like yourself, are celebrating a special occasion. Think positively about your speech and remind yourself that it's going to go just fine.

BEFORE THE SPEECH

Whatever you do, don't drink to calm your nerves before the speech! If someone suggests you get a drink down you for that reason, say no. It may seem like a good idea (especially after a couple) but it is a huge no-no. Your concentration will go out the window, so stay sober. Of course, once your speech is finished have a drink on me—you deserve it!

Before you step up to speak, try this relaxation technique:

- sit with your arms by your sides and feet firmly on the ground

- take in a big deep breath through your nose as you clench your fists, press your feet into the floor and hunch up your shoulders

- hold it for a couple of seconds then slowly exhale, at the same time slowly loosening your fists, shoulders and feet— let your stresses fall and float away as you exhale completely.

As you step up, breathe easy. If you feel your chest tensing, take in a slow, deep breath and relax it as you exhale. Then, make sure you assume a good posture (see Chapter 15 on body language). Before speaking, slowly and calmly look around the room as you would when meeting up with friends. Give the crowd a welcoming smile.

DURING THE SPEECH

- If your mouth starts to go dry, take a sip of water. If there isn't any nearby, use an old trick of imagining you are sucking a juicy orange or an ice-block (ice-pop).

- If there are any interruptions such as a fork falling onto the floor or a chair being moved, ignore it. These are normal sounds during any wedding speech.

- If you hear some people talking or whispering in the room, don't let it get to you. If someone is talking during a speech that's simply their poor manners—concentrate on your words.

- If you pop a joke out and no-one really laughs, don't try to rescue it or start again. Move on or make a joke out of it with a comment such as, 'I thought it was a dumb joke as well.'

- If someone starts heckling you (in good nature) pause right there. Let them throw a quick line (it is usually funny anyway). You can always use a good reply I heard once from a speaker, 'I thought the point of heckling was to make the speaker look like an idiot, not the heckler.'

- If you get lost in your words, don't panic just cover up with a cough and refer to your cue card again. What was the last part you said? Just like finding keys, think about when you came in the door, where did you put them?

FINAL WORDS OF ADVICE

There are three final rules you need to know to deliver a great speech: practice, practice, practice! Overkill? Not at all. If you know your material, the rest spreads like soft butter on warm toast.

To check on your speaking voice, practice and have someone listen to your speech. Also record and play it back to listen for any flaws (don't be afraid to change words in your speech script). To check on your gestures and posture, practice in front of a long mirror or even video tape yourself.

Practice as regularly as you can. What you are aiming for is to know the speech almost off the top of your head. Don't forget, you need to practice the final script of the speech so that you can simply rely on the cue card on the night.

Finally, good luck with your speech. Everyone is capable of more than they believe. So, step up, say your piece and enjoy the moment!

NOTES

OTHER WEDDING TITLES
BY NEW HOLLAND PUBLISHERS

The Complete Wedding Handbook by David Holmsen

Simple and Stylish Weddings by Jo Rigg

Wedding Journal

First published in 2004 by New Holland Publishers
London • Sydney • Auckland

Bentinck House, 3–8 Bolsover Street, London W1W 6AB, UK
1/66 Gibbes Street, Chatswood, NSW 2067, Australia
5/39 Woodside Ave, Northcote, Auckland 0627, New Zealand

newhollandpublishers.com

A record of this book is held at the British Library and the National Library
of Australia.

ISBN 9781741101119

Group Managing Director: Fiona Schultz
Publisher: Fiona Schultz
Project Editor: Liz Hardy
Designer: Yolanda La Gorcé
Production Director: Arlene Gippert
Printer: Toppan Leefung Printing Limited

10 9 8 7 6 5 4 3

Keep up with New Holland Publishers on Facebook
facebook.com/NewHollandPublishers

UK £6.99
US $9.99